SELF-DEVELOPMENT FOR SUCCESS

Time management

Acknowledgements

In writing this book, my thanks go mainly to my husband, Ron, for his patience, support, and practical help in reading and editing the text for grammatical errors. Also, his understanding of my emotional needs during the periods of writing, which made heavy demands on my mental and physical energy, have been unfailing. All of this was fitted into an already demanding work schedule.

Also, thanks go to Bernard Burgess for his thoughts and ideas, which have been incorporated into the text.

Finally, thanks to Bozena Krahn from Bank Handlowy w Warszawie SA, London, and Hilary English of City Personnel Goup, London, without whom this book would never have been written.

SELF-DEVELOPMENT FOR SUCCESS

Time management

THE ESSENTIAL GUIDE TO THINKING AND WORKING SMARTER

Katie Jones

AMERICAN MANAGEMENT ASSOCIATION

AMACOM
American Management Association
New York • Atlanta • Boston • Chicago • Kansas City
San Francisco • Washington, D. C.
Brussels • Mexico City • Tokyo • Toronto

A Marshall Edition
Conceived, edited, and designed by
Marshall Editions Ltd.
The Orangery, 161 New Bond Street
London W1Y 9PA

This book is available at a special discount when ordered in bulk quantities. For information, contact Special Sales Department, AMACOM, an imprint of AMA Publications, a division of American Management Association,1601 Broadway, New York, NY 10019.

This publication is designed to provide accurate and authoritative information in regard to the subject matter covered. It is sold with the understanding that the publisher is not engaged in rendering legal, accounting, or other professional service. If legal advice or other expert assistance is required, the services of a competent professional person should be sought.

Library of Congress Cataloging-in-Publication Data
Jones, Katie, 1947–
    Time management / Katie Jones.
        p. cm.
    Includes biographical references and index.
    ISBN 0-8144-7018-1
    1. Time management.   I Title.
HD69.T54J664 1999
650.1--dc21   98-53808
                                                          CIP

Printing number

10 9 8 7 6 5 4 3 2 1

Series Consultant Editor Chris Roebuck
Project Editor Conor Kilgallon
Designer Balley Design Associates
Art Director Sean Keogh
Managing Art Editor Patrick Carpenter
Managing Editor Clare Currie
Editorial Assistant Sophie Sandy
Editorial Coordinator Rebecca Clunes
Production Nikki Ingram

Cover photography The Stock Market

Originated in Italy by Articolor
Printed and bound in Portugal by Printer Portuguesa

Contents

1

What is time management?
Goals
Benefits

A precious resource
Reducing stress
Problem solver

What is time management?

What do you really want to do?

The one thing everyone has in common is that we all have 24 hours in a day, seven days in a week, and 52 weeks in a year.

Time is a precious resource that cannot be replaced. Once spent, it is gone forever. A bit dramatic? Not really, our ability to manage our time is the ONE thing that will make a difference to what we achieve in life.

Imagine yourself in your seventies or eighties, looking back on your life, thinking about the past. It is very unlikely that you would think about the things you did in your life; it is far more likely that you will be thinking about those things you didn't do, that you would really have liked to have accomplished. Your thoughts are likely to be, "If only I'd… learned another language, played a musical instrument, visited certain countries on vacation, learned to sail, gone scuba-diving, treated the children and grandchildren to that special holiday."

This is an excellent exercise to really concentrate the mind on what we would like to achieve in life, before it's too late. So I would encourage you to do this, right now. Do some daydreaming, allow your mind to wander, and your subconscious will come up with those things you would really, really like to do. This will become important later on in the book when you are doing other exercises to establish what your priorities are and how you should allocate your time.

Long-term satisfaction

Time management is the ability to decide what is important in life, both at work and in our home and personal lives and to prioritize certain jobs so that we complete the tasks we need to, as well as those that we think are really important. Many people spend more time planning their next vacation, than planning their lives. Just think which is likely to give you more long-term satisfaction.

Planning our lives – deciding what job we want to do, what change of direction we could make in our career, or what other goals we would like to achieve – can provide us with more satisfaction. It helps us to feel good about ourselves – on an ongoing basis, rather than just for two weeks of the year.

The ability to manage our time is an important life skill. Once we provide our minds with goals to aim for, they will start to work on ways of achieving those goals; and we will find that opportunities come our way.

Why is time management important?

Good time management provides us with the ability to keep a balance in our lives or to recognize where the imbalance is. For instance, is all of our focus on work, rather than on leisure and social activities? What about our family and those near and dear to us? Are they allowed to play an important role in our lives, or are they constantly brushed to one side?

In my experience, time management is one of those skills that many people have to work hard at; however, the benefits are plain to see. It is a skill that can be learned, practiced, and improved upon all the time. It enables us to fix our undivided attention on what needs to be done and takes away the stress of having things going round and round in our minds, thus releasing energy to concentrate on the job at hand. I have found, even in straightforward matters, such as entertaining friends at dinner, that using a simple list ensures everything is done in good time and, more importantly, that nothing is overlooked.

It is a skill everyone needs. Unfortunately, not everyone will acquire it; and as a result they will achieve less in their lives than they are capable of. The fact that you have bought, and are still reading, this book proves that you don't want to let that happen!

A precious resource

Time is the most precious resource we have because once we have spent it, unlike money, it is gone forever. You may be thinking that once money is spent, it is also gone forever. The difference is that you can never relive yesterday, whereas you can always earn more money.

There is a saying that emphasizes the importance of managing our time: "Time flies. Are you the pilot or the passenger?" Are you maximizing what you do with your time, or are you allowing yourself to drift along with whatever happens to be going on, hoping that you will enjoy it? When you think about time, think about it as a budget item – an expensive one. If you have ever found yourself thinking "I'm too busy," I have another thought for you: Too busy is a state of mind, and it can become a habit.

It is just possible that making the decision to manage your time better from now on will be the most dramatic step you'll ever take to improve your life (and a comparatively easy one after reading this book and doing the exercises). It will enable you to live life to the fullest, enjoy yourself, and feel good because you will know where you are going and how you are going to get there! So go on; don't procrastinate any further: DO IT NOW – MAKE THAT DECISION!

Setting goals

We can achieve a greater feeling of balance in our lives when we set some realistic goals for ourselves. These goals should encompass our whole lives, not just our professional circumstances. They should also enable us to prioritize our time, because once we have these goals in front of us, we can see what steps are necessary to allow us to reach our destination. Our goals can be broken down into various categories: professional, home and family, social, leisure, friends, holidays, hobbies, and personal development, such as learning a new language and even developing our time-management skills.

Goals provide our minds with a focus; and, once they have a focus, it is amazing what we can achieve. Once you set yourself goals to achieve, all kinds of circumstances will present themselves, almost as if by magic, which will enable you to move towards success. You might be thinking at this stage that there are so many things you want in life that the task is too daunting, and you would prefer not to embark on it. But it is far better to identify a long list of goals and succeed in some of them, than to identify none and achieve nothing. That can only end in frustration, a sense of demoralisation, and disappointment.

Once you have set your goals, the next stage is to make an action plan that breaks the task down into manageable "bite-size" chunks. Then you can move towards those goals, one step at a time. It is important to place an expected time limit on completing that part of the plan. Once you take this step, you can monitor your progress and see whether you are on track or whether you have set yourself too ambitious a target. Motivating yourself in this way will provide you with energy because you will feel good about the progress you are making. Without any goals on which to focus, we tend to drift through life, aimlessly allowing life to "happen" to us. This is when we experience the feeling of life controlling us and it being "unfair." You have the ability within you to do and achieve whatever you want. The first step is to determine what you want to do with your life. We will return to the subject of goals later in the book when we look at how to impove your time management.

Motivation and rewards

The other benefit of goal setting is the feeling of motivation you experience. Once you get started and can see that, by accomplishing a little at a time, you are on the way to achieving something much bigger and better in your life. It is also important to give yourself some rewards as you progress so that, as you complete certain stages toward a particular goal, you know what reward you will receive. It is important that the reward is proportionate to what you have achieved. For example, if you were learning a new language at night school, you could reward yourself on completing the first term by buying some new clothes. A vacation would be the reward for completing the course and would have the added benefit of providing you with an opportunity to speak the new language.

Goals pie chart

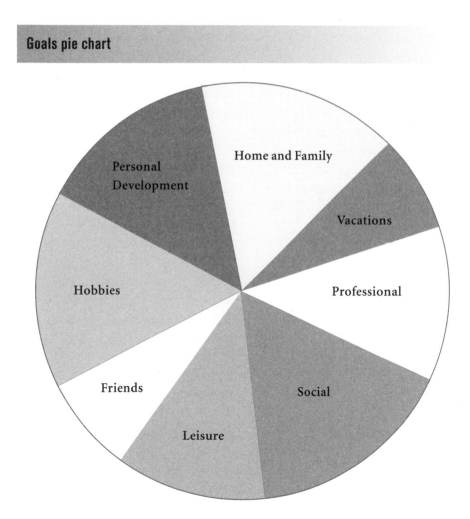

What are the benefits?

There are many benefits, some of which we have already touched upon. However, let's just list a few of them right now; and you will almost certainly be able to add some of your own! You will:

- Achieve more at work, at home, and in your leisure time
- Live a more balanced life
- Reduce the stress in your life
- Have more energy
- Be more self-disciplined
- Have more focus to concentrate your efforts
- Have more motivation to achieve what you want
- Enjoy more success in your career
- Increase your self-esteem and belief in yourself
- Have greater motivation – move to "I can" rather than "I can't" thinking

- Better able to work on key result areas
- Better able to control interruptions
- Better able to concentrate
- Better able to avoid procrastination
- Better able to run effective meetings
- More capable of achieving good team spirit

Professional benefits

I have shown above some personal benefits. Let us now look at the benefits in your professional life. If you are good at managing your time, you will become:

- More reliable
- More productive
- More able to exploit career opportunities
- More organized in your work methods
- Better able to delegate

Benefits to others

Having the ability to manage your time not only has benefits for you, as you can see from the above list, but it can also have tremendous benefits for other people. These can include:

- Improvements in everyone's time management
- Improvement of overall discipline
- More productive use of other people's time
- The setting of good examples
- Through delegation, a general improvement in responsibility and skills development
- Improved knowledge and understanding of where people stand and what is expected of them

Reducing stress

It is well recognized that managing time efficiently is one of the major factors in reducing stress. Stress is often a result of feeling out of control, either at work or at home or both. There are situations we experience in life that are clearly very stressful, such as marriage, bereavement, divorce, and moving. However, again, if we use our time-management principles and plan what we are going to do, we put a focus back into our lives. This enables us to move forward more quickly and return to enjoying life to the fullest.

Once you have reached a high level of stress, there is every likelihood you will experience serious health problems. Even before that, if you are suffering from stress, you are more vulnerable to all the germs and viruses that are always around us. This is another extremely good reason to make a decision NOW to improve your time-management skills.

Some situations that can cause you to feel stress are:

- Too much work and not enough time in which to complete it
- Delays, whether avoidable or not, which leave you feeling angry and frustrated
- Rushing around trying to do everything at twice your normal rate
- An inability to switch off once you are at home
- Finding it difficult or impossible to relax when on vacation
- Becoming impatient with others when they are slow at grasping things
- Believing you need tight deadlines before you can get motivated

Where does it all go wrong?

Problem areas

Time management can go wrong for all kinds of reasons, particularly a lack of understanding of the major difference it can make to the quality of our lives.

Many people are sent to time-management seminars by their employers. There, they take in all the information in the course; but, once they go back to work, they quickly fall back into their old ways. Either, they lack the commitment to make some changes in their lives or they fail to see the benefits available to them. There are others who fail to see the importance of delegating because they believe "No one will do it as well as I can," or "You can't trust other people to get it right, and I'd only have to clear up the problems afterward." We will look at delegation later in the book and see that there are some simple rules which, if applied properly, contradict the remarks above.

Until you start to log how you spend your time, it is difficult to answer the question, "Where does it go wrong?" Later on in the book there will be examples of time logs. Until then, we can note that there are two key areas where time just disappears: on the telephone and at meetings. How disciplined are you when you use the telephone? There are some steps you can take to help you to be more focused when making phone calls, without

> Like any other new skill, time management has to be practised on a regular basis before it becomes a habit. How long does it take to develop a new habit? Between 21 and 30 days, if the new habit is used on a daily basis.

being rude or abrupt. A poorly run meeting is another situation that often is a timewaster. Do you need to be there for the whole meeting, or could you just attend part of it? Do meetings start on time? Is an agenda used? Does everyone concerned have an opportunity to contribute to the agenda? Do you prepare before going to a meeting so that you can be succinct in putting your points forward? Does everyone involved understand all the topics on the agenda?

Patience and practice

Many people want to see "instant" results, but this is not always possible. When you are developing a new skill, you need to be patient and experiment with the basic principles until you achieve a format that works for you. Part of any new learning process involves taking time to reflect on what you have learned and what the advantages and disadvantages are. The way you learn can have an impact on this process. Some people learn in a very hands-on way, so the task of reflecting on what they have already done may be a complete turn-off. Others are only convinced if they can see immediately that there are benefits to putting new ideas into practice. There will be more about the way you learn later in the book, which will help you to identify your learning patterns and the likely stumbling blocks.

For others, the difficulty in learning time management lies in the sheer discipline required to put something new into practice. These people have become so caught up in their comfort zone that only a major event will shift their attitudes. The fact that you are reading this book suggests that you are not in this category.

Where do you go from here?

Now that you have an overview of the main aspects of time management, we can begin to develop ideas in more depth. In order to move forward, first you need to know where you are at the moment.

The middle section of this book is designed to help you understand yourself better through a series of questionnaires on the quality of your present time management and work methods. Self-knowledge and awareness are two of the most valuable assets you can develop. Developing them is not always a comfortable process, but by becoming aware of your weaknesses you will provide yourself with tremendous insight and opportunities for personal growth.

At this point, I would encourage you to take time to reflect as you work through the next section. It is designed to help you review what you have learnt so far and to enable you to understand how this will be useful to you in your quest to improve your life skill of time management.

Once you have completed the exercises, it would be useful for you to come back to these pages and compare what the exercises have revealed to you about yourself with the way you previously perceived yourself.

Problem Solver

1. What have been the main points that have had an impact on you in this first chapter?

_____

_____

_____

_____

_____

_____

2. To what extent do you feel committed to experiment with the new ideas and principles that will follow in the next chapters?

_____

_____

_____

_____

3. What areas of your life would you like to reorganize so that you would feel less pressured and more in control of your life?

_____

_____

_____

_____

Problem Solver

4. How rigid or relaxed are you in planning your life at the moment?

_____

_____

_____

_____

_____

5. Do you review your life on a regular basis to check where you are going and how you are doing?

_____

_____

_____

_____

6. What goals have you set yourself in (a) the past? (b) for the future?

_____

_____

_____

_____

2

Assessing yourself
Time wasting
Procrastination
Perfectionism

Questionnaires
Personal reviews
Putting the knowledge together

Self-assessment: where am I now?

We ended the last chapter by assessing some aspects of your life so far and by thinking about some of the points covered in the chapter. These ideas may not have been new to you, but perhaps I have brought them back into focus.

The questions were designed to help you think about your life and to consider how disciplined you are already. Don't worry if you did not like the answers. We all have room for improvement, and honesty is the most sensible approach. Ultimately, there is no point in deluding ourselves.

Time management can be defined as being EFFECTIVE (carrying out the right tasks at the right times), rather than being EFFICIENT (doing tasks well). Although there will be different problems for every individual, there are some common difficulties running through many work situations. These difficulties often become apparent in planning, completing work, and relating to people. Examples include:

- Having too much work and not enough time to do it
- Working beyond normal working hours
- Staff not trained properly
- Deadlines not being met
- Meetings running longer than necessary
- Danger of work compromising private and social life
- Interruptions and disturbances
- Unexpected crises
- Time spent traveling to meetings and appointments
- General lack of control and discipline
- Lack of training in new technology
- Feeling under pressure to take work home

Questionnaires

The following questionnaire will enable you to assess your particular ability to manage time. When a business is being assessed, the starting point has to be, "Where is it now?" This approach is adopted here also so that you can see where your current skill level is and identify the areas in which you need work. Then there are some other questionnaires on the specific aspects of how time can "disappear" because of a desire to be "perfect" or, at the other end of the scale, a tendency to "procrastinate." Even if you don't fall into either of these camps, work through the questions anyway. Procrastination is a problem many people can identify with, while the desire to be perfect leads others to feel constant pressure.

Take a few minutes to look again at the opposite list and check those that apply to you. From those you have marked, decide whether there is a common thread, i.e., Is it about your ability to manage yourself through your planning (or lack of it)? Is it about your ability to manage other people and the skills you need to do that? When you have responsibility for other people on a team, you need to plan and organize others, delegate work, monitor progress, and discuss objectives with individuals. As a manager or supervisor, there are three important areas to focus on. They are:

- **The tasks that have to be achieved**
- **The team that is available to do that**
- **The needs of each individual on the team**

When we have a clear idea of what needs to be achieved and understand the strengths of our team – taking into consideration the needs and aspirations of the individuals involved – we will find that the tasks are achieved much more easily, either ahead of or at the very least, on time.

How do you manage time now?

Check your existing skills

For each question, tick the response which is closest to the truth:

1 How good are you at managing your time now?
- [ ] Very good: my ability to manage my time is not a problem
- [ ] All right, although I am sometimes under pressure
- [ ] I feel I am always under pressure
- [ ] My life feels out of balance, all work and no play
- [ ] My work is my whole life, so I concentrate on that alone

2 Do you set clear goals and objectives for each day?
- [ ] Yes
- [ ] More often than not
- [ ] No

3 Do you complete your daily goals and objectives?
- [ ] Yes
- [ ] More often than not
- [ ] No

4 Do you know where you lose time during your day?
- [ ] Always
- [ ] Never
- [ ] Uncertain

5 Are you aware of your "prime time" – that part of the day when you carry out your most important tasks?
- [ ] Always
- [ ] Never
- [ ] Sometimes

6 When you are making a list of things to do, do you prioritize the tasks?
- [ ] Yes
- [ ] More often than not
- [ ] No

7 Do you consider different methods of communicating something and then choose the most efficient one for the task?
- [ ] Always
- [ ] Never
- [ ] Uncertain
- [ ] Variable

Check your existing skills

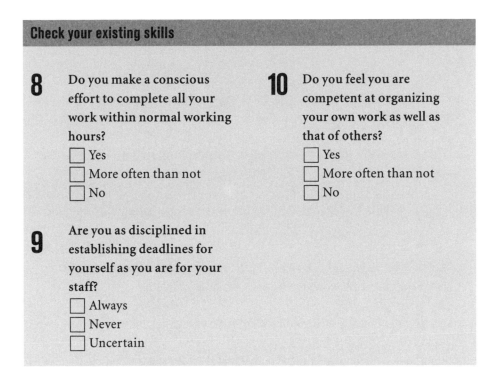

8 Do you make a conscious effort to complete all your work within normal working hours?

- ☐ Yes
- ☐ More often than not
- ☐ No

9 Are you as disciplined in establishing deadlines for yourself as you are for your staff?

- ☐ Always
- ☐ Never
- ☐ Uncertain

10 Do you feel you are competent at organizing your own work as well as that of others?

- ☐ Yes
- ☐ More often than not
- ☐ No

How do you manage time now?

PERSONAL REVIEW USING RESULTS FROM THE QUESTIONNAIRE

1. What have you learned about yourself and your current level of ability to manage your time?

2. What areas would you like to improve in the next three months? (Set yourself a maximum of three areas to work on at any one time.)

3. Make a list of activities where you currently lose time during your working day (and at home as well, if you wish).

4. What are the main tasks you have to carry out in order to meet your own work objectives? (Your job description will help you here.)

5. How do you currently go about deciding which tasks take priority?

6. When you communicate with colleagues, staff, customers, etc., what methods do you currently use?

7. Are there more efficient ways of doing this? List what has to be communicated and how you have done that up to now.

8. At what time of day do you feel the most energetic and mentally alert?

9. What types of tasks do you carry out when you are like this?

Having answered the questions above, you will now have an overview of your ability to manage your time. Using your answers as a starting point, there are now some more specific issues to focus on – your Time Wasters (the common ways in which you personally waste time).

Aims

In order to arrive at the stage where we feel we are living a balanced life and have control over it, our aim is to achieve the following:

■ Compile a daily list of tasks to be achieved. If you regularly find you have not achieved everything on your list, review how much you are putting on the list, or consider delegating some tasks. To fall short of your expectations on a regular basis will have a de-moralising effect – the complete opposite of what good time management is intended to do.

■ The process of prioritizing keeps you focused on what is important. These tasks will usually relate to your longer-term goals. On a daily basis, you will be faced with tasks that might appear important and need to be done now. The question to ask yourself is, "how does this fit into the big picture?"

■ As a manager or supervisor, people in your team will have expectations of you, part of which will be about leading by example. This means you must set deadlines for yourself that you can achieve and perhaps even exceed. In order to be successful, part of the process is having the ability to plan and organize your own workload so that sufficient chunks of time are allocated to the important tasks. You will also set a good example by completing what needs to be done within the normal working day.

Being very aware of how you use your time is the key to continually improving the way you work. Only in exceptional circumstances should you be taking work home.

■ The methods of communication you choose will depend on what needs to be done and can have a major impact on your daily achievements. Adopting habits, such as allocating time slots for phone calls, is very useful, so you will be mentally in gear for doing these tasks. The use of e-mail has revolutionised the speed at which people communicate. Not only is it quick, it is much cheaper than other methods.

If you who need to have face-to-face meetings with customers or suppliers, set an objective for the meeting to keep you focused. If such meetings are away from your normal place of work, always endeavor to have other meetings in the area on the same day so you economize on your travel time and costs.

Time wasters

Let's look at time wasters. These are listed under different categories. Work through each category in turn, and when you agree with a particular statement, put a check in the appropriate box. If you don't agree with a statement, just leave the box blank.

1   Ability to be disciplined in my work   **I agree**

I don't make lists of jobs to be done.   ☐
I don't set goals/targets for myself.   ☐
I do set goals/targets but then don't use them.   ☐
I like to talk to others, often interrupting their work.   ☐
My concentration levels are poor, and I am easily
distracted.   ☐
I frequently try to do several tasks at once.   ☐
I like to be involved in everything.   ☐
I frequently make social telephone calls from work.   ☐

2   Ability to say "no"

I enjoy helping others.   ☐
I like to do things that make me feel important.   ☐
I do not like to think I have upset other people.   ☐
I would much rather say "Yes" than "No."   ☐
I find I am often interrupted at work.   ☐
I tend to agree to deadlines that I doubt I can meet.   ☐
I find it difficult to keep meetings with visitors brief,
even when they are unscheduled.   ☐
I tend to deal with low-priority requests or projects
in preference to the task I am working on, even if I
know that they are less important.   ☐

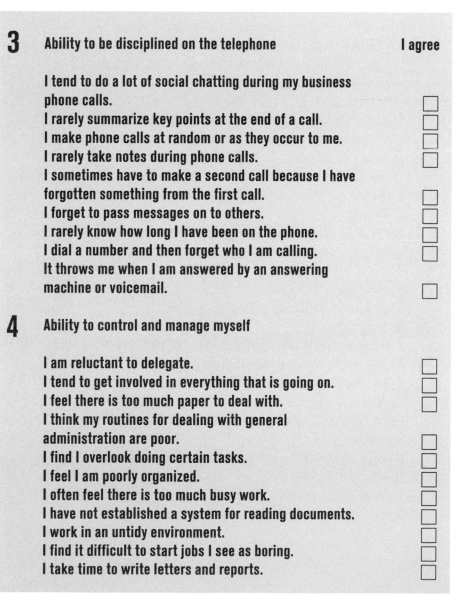

3   **Ability to be disciplined on the telephone**   **I agree**

I tend to do a lot of social chatting during my business
phone calls. ☐
I rarely summarize key points at the end of a call. ☐
I make phone calls at random or as they occur to me. ☐
I rarely take notes during phone calls. ☐
I sometimes have to make a second call because I have
forgotten something from the first call. ☐
I forget to pass messages on to others. ☐
I rarely know how long I have been on the phone. ☐
I dial a number and then forget who I am calling. ☐
It throws me when I am answered by an answering
machine or voicemail. ☐

4   **Ability to control and manage myself**

I am reluctant to delegate. ☐
I tend to get involved in everything that is going on. ☐
I feel there is too much paper to deal with. ☐
I think my routines for dealing with general
administration are poor. ☐
I find I overlook doing certain tasks. ☐
I feel I am poorly organized. ☐
I often feel there is too much busy work. ☐
I have not established a system for reading documents. ☐
I work in an untidy environment. ☐
I find it difficult to start jobs I see as boring. ☐
I take time to write letters and reports. ☐

Time wasters

5   **Ability to communicate well**   **I agree**

I tend to just say what I want to say, when I want to say it. ☐
I consider only what my needs for information are likely
to be, rather than other people's. ☐
I often think that other departments are interested only
in their own problems. ☐
I often find other people don't reply to my requests. ☐
Other people do not seem to understand my priorities. ☐
Telling people what I need seems to take a long time,
so often I don't bother. ☐
I think people should know what my priorities and
needs are. ☐

6   **Ability to be disciplined at meetings,**
including informal ones with only one other person

I lack an agenda and time lines for each topic. ☐
Often there is no clearly defined purpose for the
meeting. ☐
Sometimes people who attend don't need to be there. ☐
People frequently go off on tangents. ☐
I often find there are points I want to get across, but I
don't get the opportunity. ☐
There are often several people talking at once, so points
are missed. ☐
It takes a long time to circulate minutes from the
meeting. ☐
No clear action plans result from the meeting. ☐
No one ever seems to follow up on action plans
identified. ☐

7   **Ability to review systems and procedures**   **I agree**

My desk is often a mess. ☐
There is no clearly defined procedure for dealing with messages. ☐
Information is not filed away on a regular basis. ☐
I am unaware of my boss's priorities on either a daily or
weekly basis. ☐
I am unaware of what people do in other areas within
the company. ☐
I spend time looking for things on my desk/work space. ☐
I often have difficulty deciding what tasks to do first. ☐

Now you have completed this "Time Waster" exercise and learned
more about yourself, the next review section will enable you to put the
points into an ordered framework. This will give you a list of the areas
you should work on in order to feel you are more in control and under
less pressure.

Time wasters

TIME WASTERS REVIEW

1. What are the areas you need to work on? List them, and prioritize those that you believe will have the biggest impact on your working day.

2. Is there one particular section, such as "Ability to say no," which has more checks than any of the others? If so, which one?

3. Why are these aspects causing you a problem?

4. What actions will you take to improve in these areas?

5. What will be the benefits to you?

It's now time to move on to another subject that is a common problem for many people – procrastination – putting off until tomorrow what you could do today.

Take a step back

The importance of this section cannot be overemphasized. Most people waste time during their lives; it is the extent to which it happens that is important. It is very easy to be caught up in daily events at work, even though you know you have piles of work to do. You slog away at it day in and day out and yet never feel you are making any progress.

The only way you can change the way you work is to take a step back, review what you currently do, and then decide what changes you can make to become more effective. It is not a question of making change for the sake of change. Instead, you need to make changes to reap the benefits of rethinking the way you live, reducing your stress levels, and living a more balanced life.

The questionnaire you have just completed focuses on some very specific ways in which you work and how time is lost as a result. By increasing your awareness of the problems that waste your time, you are then in a position to make some choices. Then you can decide which areas to tackle first in order to gain the most benefits. It is worth looking at the headings, rather than the specific points under each heading, to gain a better understanding of what you must do and how to improve your ability to do it.

Remember, you are the person who will gain most by doing this review and making some changes in the way you work. It is also much easier when you have some hard evidence to help you decide what it is that needs changing.

The following questionnaire enables you to review how you work and how strong your tendency is to procrastinate. It is important that you are honest in answering these questions.

Procrastination

Think about each of the scenarios below and put a check in the column for the number that is closest to how you usually work.

As before, there are no right or wrong answers in this questionnaire. The aim is to help you identify how likely you are to procrastinate.

Statement	1	2	3	4	5	Statement
1a I regularly clear my workspace when starting a complicated job.						**1b** When I embark on a complicated job, I usually leave my desk as it is, even if it is untidy.
2a When a complicated task is progressing well I still have doubts whether it will be completed on time.						**2b** I always feel certain that my approach to a job will lead to a satisfactory outcome.
3a I frequently delay implementing useful plans I have made.						**3b** I always enjoy putting my plans into action as soon as I can.
4a I frequently can be found chatting, gossiping, or flirting with people at work.						**4b** I am focused on what needs to be done at work so that I can complete jobs. Walking around chatting to people is part of other necessary discussions.
5a The concentration and discipline to begin a job are always hard for me.						**5b** I enjoy starting on new jobs and find it easy, so I like to start them immediately.
6a There are times when I will do anything rather than face situations that involve conflict or are unfamiliar.						**6b** While I do not enjoy conflict or unfamiliar situations, I will face them and then move on.

	Statement	1	2	3	4	5		Statement
7a	I often complete low-priority jobs before high-priority jobs, even though I know there is a price to pay for doing so.						**7b**	I always complete high-priority jobs before low-priority jobs, unless there is a very good reason to do otherwise.
8a	The fear of being wrong or making mistakes means I will often put off doing a task.						**8b**	The thought of making mistakes or being wrong does not affect my ability to undertake task.
9a	Time limits for completion of tasks are usually missed because I have put off doing the tasks.						**9b**	Time limits for completion are usually met because I work towards them systematically.
10a	I leave difficult tasks until the last minute, and then panic when I have to finish them.						**10b**	I divide difficult tasks into manageable chunks so that I can do them a bit at a time.

Scoring interpretation

Having checked a number for each situation on the worksheet, add up the numbers and divide by 10.

1.0 to 1.4

You are very likely to procrastinate; your achievements are seriously impaired.

1.5 to 2.4

There is a strong likelihood that you often procrastinate; you are performing below your potential.

2.5 to 3.5

You are fully aware of your tendency to procrastinate; you work hard to control it and to keep your performance up to your potential.

3.6 to 4.5

Your tendency to procrastinate is low; your performance is not impaired.

4.6 to 5.0

You are very unlikely to procrastinate; your performance is high.

Procrastination

PROCRASTINATION REVIEW

As with other aspects of time management, the next stage is to look at yourself very specifically and identify the areas you want to improve.

1. List those aspects for which you scored 3 or less on the above questionnaire.

2. If there are more than three, then prioritize the three that will have a major impact on your job performance.

3. List four or five tasks that you know you have been putting off. They may be specific tasks that have been hanging over your head for some time, or they may be tasks you know you habitually put off doing.

4. Now list the actions you need to take for each task in order to move it forward.

Circumstances

Many people have a tendency to procrastinate, and different circumstances will affect people differently. The most important fact to learn is that you can develop new habits to overcome procrastination. The result of this is that you move into higher levels of achievement, satisfaction, and increased self-belief and self-esteem.

By completing this questionnaire, you will have a better idea of what causes you to procrastinate as well as the areas you need to work on to overcome the problem.

The main areas that are likely to emerge after you complete this questionnaire will be one or more of the following:

■ Complicated tasks
■ Your preference to socialize rather than do your job
■ Concentration and self-discipline
■ The prospect of conflict
■ Unfamiliarity with the task
■ Wanting to stay in your comfort zone, rather than stepping outside of it
■ Fear of making mistakes

The question to ask yourself is whether it is one factor or a combination of factors that cause you to put off doing your important tasks.

Overcoming procrastination

Establish in your own mind why you are procrastinating. Is the job not particularly important? Then, either do it quickly, or get rid of it. If the timing is awkward, decide when you can do it, and add it to your "To do" list.

Do the unpleasant tasks first. When you have done these, you will be in a positive frame of mind and more motivated to do the other tasks. Having unpleasant tasks hanging over your head for days or weeks on end saps your vital energy and causes considerable anxiety. Develop a new habit of always doing the unpleasant tasks first.

Break up large tasks or projects into bite-sized chunks that are manageable. Put these on to your action plan, and prioritize them; some parts will depend on doing other parts first. This will ensure that the whole task is completed on time.

Checklist:

Find instant tasks to start you off, those which take five minutes or less. Instant tasks may include:

■ **Gathering all the papers related to a project in one file so that everything is ready for you to start.**

■ **Reading important documents related to the task first.**

■ **Making a list of people who may be involved in the project – their names, their potential roles, and their telephone numbers.**

■ **Talking to a colleague about ideas on how to get into the project.**

Do I demand a perfect job every time?

The next questionnaire logically follows the last one because the desire to do a perfect job all the time can often cause us to procrastinate. If we don't seem to have enough time to do the job to the highest possible standard, we will often put off even attempting it. The end result is that when we must do the work, we find ourselves under tremendous pressure and may even take it home with us.

The purpose of this book is to help you move away from such habits by being more disciplined in your approach and, at times, expecting less of yourself. Sometimes doing 80 or 90 percent of a job is sufficient, and it is not necessary to add that extra 10 percent of detail to make it perfect. If you have a tendency to want to do a perfect job, this may well be the most difficult habit to change. However, for your own sanity, it is important that you work on it. For many people this tendency finds its roots in childhood, when demanding parents insisted on perfection before saying, "Well done" or giving an approving pat on the back.

Here is the next assessment to help you to identify how strong your desire is to do a perfect job every time. Circle the number that best describes you.

Scoring system:

This is not typical of me: score 1 point
I am like this sometimes: score 2 points
This is typical of me: score 3 points

I rely only on myself to get a job done properly.	1	2	3
My personal standards are very high, and I will not accept anything less.	1	2	3
I generally prepare several drafts of reports and letters.	1	2	3
I often miss deadlines because the work has not come up to my high standards.	1	2	3

I frequently find fault with colleagues and family.	1	2	3
When I go over work I have already done, I usually have to make alterations.	1	2	3
Tasks that need in-depth information often cause me to feel "beaten."	1	2	3
I am always concerned about making errors; it is unacceptable to me and others.	1	2	3
Members of my team get frustrated because their work has not come up to my high standards.	1	2	3
I am reluctant to ask for help.	1	2	3
I am reluctant to delegate jobs to other people because I still have to watch over them and check what they do.	1	2	3
When I doubt my ability to complete a job to a high standard, I don't start it.	1	2	3
		Total	☐

Scoring

Add up your score, and write it in the box. If your score is more than 24, you may be too much of a perfectionist. In other words, you are hung up on getting everything exactly right every time. However, few tasks ever turn out exactly as you would like. Once you can accept this, you will reduce the amount of time you waste.

Do I demand a perfect job every time?

PERFECTIONISM REVIEW

1. If my score is more than 24 on this questionnaire, what are the implications for me at work and in my life generally?

2. Of those questions on which I have scored either 2 or 3, which are the most important to work on?

3. What actions should I take in order to make improvements to these areas?

4. When we are striving to make changes in our lives, it helps if we have someone who can support us and make helpful suggestions. Who will I choose to help support me through this?

5. What rewards will there be for me?

Unrealistic expectations

Being a perfectionist may seem very laudable to you. However, in truth, it is also an unrealistic expectation to set for yourself. There are certain jobs that may need to be completed to the highest standard. One that comes to mind is decorating and, in particular, wallpapering. If that is not done properly, the evidence is there for you to see as a constant reminder.

A working environment is rarely like hanging wallpaper. Projects move forward and are finished; then it is time to move on to the next one. There are times when the current project is not even finished or the criteria have all changed, making it effectively a new project.

By completing this questionnaire, you may have discovered that perfectionism is not a problem for you, in which case you can move on. If your score is over 24, you need to consider the pressure you put on yourself and whether it will bring about any major improvements in the long run.

Perfectionism can lead you to do some, or all, of the following:

- Unnecessary reviews and rewrites of work that should have been already finished or of work that you have delegated to other members in your team.
- Unnecessary and unwarranted criticism of colleagues at work and family members, which leads to increased strain on working and/or family relationships.
- Having people unwilling to offer any help if you have a high workload, either because of previous, unnecessary criticism or the demoralising effect of you having to make constant changes to their contributions.
- Procrastination, which, as we have seen from the exercise starting on page 32 ,will lead to serious time management problems.

Reassess your standards

When you start to realize there are some serious disadvantages in being a perfectionist, it makes a great deal of sense to reassess your own standards and accept that more realistic standards will satisfy the goals.

Learning to manage your time successfully is intended to help you lead a more balanced life – to allow you to spend more time with your family and follow other pursuits, such as keeping fit, hobbies, and interests that can be otherwise "left on the shelf" because you do not have the time to do them. Remember that you have 24 hours in a day, seven days in a week, and 52 weeks in a year. It is what you put into that time that counts and will make the difference to your satisfaction and contentment in life.

Putting the knowledge together

These questionnaires
have covered four
distinct areas,
which are:
■ Your general
ability to manage
time
■ What wastes
your time
■ Your inclination
to procrastinate
■ Your desire to be
perfect

As a result of doing these different questionnaires and reviewing the points that have come out of them, you are now in a much better position to understand yourself. It is important to identify those areas of time management that are currently causing you to feel pressure, stress, or lack of balance. Always rushing around is a typical example of poor time management. Rather than deciding for ourselves what we want to do and when we want to do it, we allow ourselves to be at everyone's beck and call; and this can leave us feeling exhausted.

The summaries of each of these four areas now provide you with additional information about how you currently manage your time and the problem areas that need to be addressed. The specific areas of time wasting compounded by your tendency to procrastinate and desire to be perfect, will enable you to come to grips with the problems and embark on some positive corrective action.

Some clear messages are likely to emerge from all of this information. Those messages should be looked at together to gain an understanding of the whole, rather than taking the results of each questionnaire in isolation. Among these will be some or all of the following:

■ Your ability to manage and discipline yourself
■ A lack of self-belief
■ Avoiding conflict, revealing problems in relationships with others and your ability to communicate well
■ Being highly critical of both yourself and others
■ Priorities not in line with goals and tasks; wanting a "perfect" job rather than a 'complete' job.

Depending on the amount of information you have learned about yourself, you may now be feeling that you have a mountain to climb. It is important to keep all this information in perspective, by looking at the areas that are causing you the most problems first and then gradually working on other areas as you progress and develop. This is not a "five-minute job."

Take two of the points from the list above as an example: criticism of yourself and others. The first step in solving the problem is to recognize that you do it. You could ask for feedback from people whom you trust, both at work and socially, to tell you whenever they notice that you are being critical of either yourself and others. Once you start receiving this information, it is comparatively easy to change. Be aware of the pressure you put yourself under by being critical of everything you do.

Another example is lack of self-belief, an area of personal development that will take some time to change. One very good way is to make a regular habit of reading positive mental attitude books on a daily basis – 20 minutes a day as a minimum. A number of titles on this subject are suggested at the end of this book.

Exercise

1. From the four exercises in this chapter, list all the areas you feel you would like to develop in order to be more in control of your job and your life.

_____

_____

_____

2. Summarize all the actions you have planned to take as a result of the other reviews in this chapter.

_____

_____

_____

3. Using those lists, prioritize them in order of importance using, "1" as an immediate priority, "2" as medium priority, and "3" as long-term priority.

_____

_____

_____

3

Principles of time management

Setting goals

Personal development

Coping with office procedures
Action plans and time logs
Delegation

Ways to help you get better

The purpose of this chapter is to provide you with the tools and techniques you need to improve your ability to manage your time. This will enable you to live a more controlled lifestyle with less pressure, greater flexibility, and more enjoyment. The techniques will cover the specific issues raised by the questionnaires, as well as some generally accepted basic principles of time management. First, let's take a look at some of the skills that many tasks require, in the workplace (all of these skills apply) or at home (several of these skills may apply). They are:

- Collecting information
- Communicating
- Controlling
- Being creative
- Implementing
- Monitoring
- Planning
- Setting goals/objectives
- Working with others

Collecting information

Information comes in many forms; everything that lands on your desk is information. Such items include minutes of meetings, notes from colleagues, your own reminders, publications, letters and memos, reports, telephone calls, face-to-face conversations, and computer print outs.

The problem with information is how and where to store it. You need to establish some rules regarding how long you keep information. The length of time will depend on whether your organization has a central storage system for certain items. If such a system is not in place, it might be a good idea to suggest that one be developed. It saves money if people know that certain information is available in one location. If it is information you need personally, you should decide your own guidelines. Up to one year for most items is normally sufficient, if they are not part of an ongoing project or contain information on employees who are still employed in the organization.

Communication

Clear communication is critical to getting things done properly. It has been calculated that most people spend up to 75 percent of their day communicating with others. Poor communication wastes time, as it increases the likelihood of making mistakes; incorrect assumptions; misunderstandings; and, ultimately, incorrect conclusions . This can lead to resentment, lack of understanding and direction, and low morale. To develop your communication skills, refer to the book in this series, *Effective Communication.*

Implementing, monitoring, and controlling

These three skills all interconnect, as they are three parts of the same process.

When you start any new job, there is the stage at the beginning when various parts of the job are implemented. As the job progresses, you will want to monitor it against the timescales and goals that you have set as a means of establishing whether you are on course or not.

If you are falling behind, you will need to take action to speed things up or take a step back to determine if there are other ways of doing your job in order to finish more quickly.

Consider the simple example of sending out direct mail to existing clients and new prospects. Certain steps must be completed: lists of names and addresses must be prepared, if they are not already in a database; the content of the letters must be written; and the letters must be processed and mailed.

As a manager, you would want to set time limits on each of those steps to ensure that everything is on track. Setting deadlines for the completion of each step enables you to monitor and control the results. If the processing of the letters falls behind, you might consider bringing in other people to help in order to achieve your deadline.

Working with others

"Teamwork is what makes the dream work" is a phrase that rolls nicely off the tongue. Think about what that message means: working well with others is necessary to achieve what you want in order to succeed.

"TEAM" can be written as:

T - Together
E - Everyone
A - Achieves
M - More

The benefits are tremendous, both for the organization and the individuals within it. Research has shown that companies become successful when they have:

- shared goals: everyone understands the business
- shared culture: the values that bring people together are agreed upon
- shared learning: a commitment to continuous improvement
- shared effort: a single organization driven by team flexibility
- shared information: effective communication

If you work in such an organization, consider yourself lucky. If you don't, think about what part you could play in changing some aspects of your company in order to start working towards some or all of these five areas.

The principles of time management

Let's now look at the principles of time management. These fall into a number of categories, which I will list and then take you through each one, step by step.

- ■ Establishing purpose
- ■ Setting goals
- ■ Action plans
- ■ Preparing a time log
- ■ Prioritizing tasks
- ■ Manager paper
- ■ Using the telephone
- ■ Attending and running meetings
- ■ Delegating
- ■ Researching and gathering information
- ■ Applying self-discipline

Before going any further, write down your purpose in your job.

The purpose of my job is:

We will come back to this after you have read the next paragraphs to see whether you were on the right track. Most people tend to confuse what they do on at work with the real purpose of their job.

If we use the example of a secretary, the tasks he/she undertakes include:

- ■ Typing
- ■ Taking shorthand
- ■ Making appointments for the boss
- ■ Filing
- ■ Answering letters
- ■ Finding information for meetings

A secretary's purpose is to support the manager and free up his/her time so he/she can do the primary tasks to achieve the purpose of that job. This could encompass a wide variety of roles, such as sales, marketing, production, finance, distribution, personnel, and managing the future of the company through strategic planning.

The bottom line is that most people's jobs involve helping the company make money. Depending on your role, you will either be making things happen or providing support to others who make things happen within the company.

You may be in a role that does not actually make money. However, you could almost certainly have an impact on the bottom line by looking for ways to save money. Anyone who helps the progress of the company by looking at the way jobs are done and devising a better way to do them, will be an invaluable asset to his or her employer. Have you had any good ideas recently for more effective ways of doing your job?

Just take a few minutes to think about the different areas of responsibility within your company, and then list them below:

> **What are the main areas of responsibility within my organization?**

Having looked at these main areas, where does your job fit in to the whole? Are the tasks you do completely in a supporting role, or is there an element of proactivity as well?

Tasks can be categorized in three main areas:
- Proactive
- Reactive
- Maintenance

Proactive tasks

Proactive tasks are those that will have a direct impact on moving business forward, or moving you closer to your overall goals. Those who work in sales, especially if they have the responsibility of obtaining new customers, are in a proactive role.

Let's look at another example of people who do proactive tasks – those in Human Resources. Their responsibilities are to recruit the right people for various jobs, to ensure that they are adequately trained, and to see that their potential is developed for the future.

As organizations grow and change, employees' skills must be developed to keep pace. This development may involve training in technical and interpersonal skills. Many executives seem to think that, once staff have been recruited, the proactive tasks within human resources management have been completed.

That is short-term thinking, because everyone in the workplace meets with new and different demands, and their development should reflect that reality.

The principles of time management

Reactive tasks

These are some of the everyday interruptions that can occur at work: incoming telephone calls, people wanting advice and help, crises that other people can't or won't deal with, or machinery breaking down.

These are the types of tasks that always need to be done. However, if you are aware of them and of how much time you spend on them, you can manage the amount of time you "waste" on them. Self-awareness plays an important part in self-improvement. Until you know how your time is spent, it is almost impossible to correct the problem. A time log is a useful way of monitoring what you do with your time on a daily basis.

Maintenance tasks

Maintenance tasks must be completed for the smooth running of an organization. Keeping a database up to date with new or revised information on customers and clients is a typical maintenance task. In itself, this does not achieve profit for the company; but, without such basic tasks, the whole business could grind to a halt.

Preparing the financial statements is also a maintenance task. Although financials do not contribute directly to the success of the company, they are a useful source of information that can identify areas where changes could increase profit. Such areas might be stationery costs, company cars, or heating and lighting. Once maintenance tasks that are possible sources of improving profit are identified, proactive tasks would help effect the change.

Do one thing at a time

Having recognized that there are different types of tasks, the next step is to give proactive tasks a high priority – it is the proactive tasks that move you forward and need to be given priority. It is important to be disciplined enough to finish one task before moving on the next, especially the proactive tasks, wherever possible. However, since the reactive tasks are the ones over which you have less control, sometimes you may need to deal with them immediately. For instance, if someone in your workplace has an accident, that must be dealt with immediately.

By completing one task at a time, you don't become too thinly spread. It also avoids the necessity of 'finding your place' again in a file or project. If you leave something important to deal with another task, then you have to go over information again and decide where you left off, and all of these things are very time consuming – and therefore, non-productive time.

Scheduling your time

Aim to schedule 60 per cent of your time for proactive tasks, leaving the other 40 per cent available for reactive and maintenance tasks, as well as unexpected interruptions, which may occur anyway. If they don't, that gives you some extra time to work on other priorities and get ahead of yourself. Remember, most jobs will take longer than you think they do and that will be especially true if you have never done a particular task before, because there will be an element of learning involved. Allow some margin for error when calculating deadlines; there is nearly always something which goes wrong when you least expect it. So expect the unexpected and you are less likely to be caught out. When dealing with very complicated tasks or projects, break them down into smaller chunks, so you are better able to allocate time to each part of the task, and then calculate the total time for the job. If you have been faced with a situation where your time calculation was far from reality, then take time to analyse why, so that you can learn from the situation and make sure you do not fall into the same trap a second time.

Setting goals and objectives

This is an essential part of any business strategy. A well-run business will have a written action plan so that there is a document spelling out the strategy, available for all to see. Ideally, the staff within an organization will know and be involved in the planning process and will see how the part they play helps achieve organizational goals. Unfortunately, there are many businesses around that do not feel the need nor see the importance of doing this. Staff members who are involved in what is going on will be far more committed to achieving these goals than those who are kept in the dark.

Objectives have to be set in such a way that their progress can be monitored. There are five criteria for setting objectives or goals. Use whichever word you prefer as they have virtually the same meaning.

Specific

It is important that your goal is stated in terms that are as specific as possible. Unless they are specific, it is very difficult to break them down into concrete steps that would make up the action plan. Let's use a hobby as an example. Imagine you decide you want to take up a new one, such as playing an instrument. You could say, "I want to learn to play music," which is better than just saying, "I want to do

All your objectives should be S M A R T, that is:

S – specific
M – measurable
A – attainable
R – realistic
T – timebound

Whenever you set yourself a goal or objective, make sure it has all these five elements.

something." However, it is still not specific, and it would be difficult to start on the project.

Now imagine that your objective becomes "I want to learn to play the piano" or "I want to learn to play the flute." The objective becomes more meaningful, and you can now start to decide the steps you need to take in order to achieve your goal. A goal or objective should be something that is really important to you, although there are times when people take up a hobby just to see what it is like and find themselves really hooked on it.

Work objectives could range from increasing sales by 10 percent or increasing profit by 20 percent to reducing costs by 30 percent. All of these would be specific objectives. From them, a step-by-step action plan could be developed.

Measurable

Once you have specified your goal or objective, the next step is to decide how to measure it. If it is very difficult to measure, it will be more difficult to achieve. If you were learning to play the piano, for example, the goal would be broken down into stages. You would start taking lessons – perhaps weekly – and aim to take your first exam after six months. That goal might have to be reviewed, but since it is measurable, it would be easy to see the progress being made.

People who want to lose weight provide a classic opportunity for setting a measurable goal. You will often hear them say, "I want to lose weight," or "I need to lose weight." The question is, how much? If they defined the objective as losing 7 lbs in two months, they would have a reasonable goal that could be measured.

Attainable

Using the above example, to lose 7 lbs in weight in two months is quite attainable, but to lose 7 lbs in a week would not be so easy. Even if you achieved it by going on a crash diet, the chances are you would gain weight in a short time. This demonstrates the importance of ensuring your goal is attainable.

Let's look at the example of learning to play the piano. Do you need other resources to make this happen? For example, do you have a piano or regular access to a piano?

Setting goals and objectives

Unless you do, it will be very difficult to achieve your goal. If you do not have the resources you need, your goal will be unattainable. It is replaced by a different goal, that of acquiring resources.

In the workplace, the same criteria apply. If you want to diversify into other product areas, do you have the resources to make it happen? Such resources are likely to be finances for buying machinery, staff with the right skills, and customers who want to buy the products.

Realistic

The goal you set for yourself has to be realistic. However, it should also challenge you because goals that are too easily attainable provide little motivation. Research has shown that people who are high achievers set very demanding goals for themselves.

Using our example of playing the piano, a goal of becoming a proficient pianist in one year's time might be achievable. However, if you were starting to learn to play from scratch

and wanted to become a concert pianist, you will have set an unrealistic goal.

Timebound

By putting a time limit on your goals, you reinforce the urgency of taking action – now rather than later. Time limits should be realistic in relation to other commitments and they should be flexible. Circumstances can change constantly, and sometimes we have to amend our time limit for a goal because other events interfere. There is another useful way to set goals and objectives. This is to divide them into "Why" goals, "What" goals, and "How" goals. This alternative approach to looking at goals is examined below.

"Why" goals

These goals usually relate to aspects of your non-working life, such as your family, your personal and other relationships, your health, and your spiritual needs.

"Why" goals influence your whole life because they provide the reasons for achieving other types of goals. Many people become too focused on the "what" and "how" goals and lose sight of "why" they wanted to achieve those goals in the first place.

"What" goals

This type of goal concerns your professional ambitions and may include areas of your life such as career, finances, and security. "What" goals are inextricably linked to the achievement of the "why" goals.

"How" goals

These establish how you are going to achieve the "what" goals.

Here is an example to illustrate how these three types of goals fit together. First, the "what" goals: This could be, "I want to become the top salesman in the company, increase my annual sales by 50 percent, and earn $100,000 per year."

Then, the "how" goals: "I will achieve these goals by improving my selling and people skills. I will also expand my contacts by joining various business clubs and organizations. I will send out more letters, make more sales calls, and close more contracts."

Finally, the "why" goals: "I want to achieve this to give my family complete security, to give my children the best education, and to provide the family with great vacations. I want to see myself as successful and to increase my self-esteem by feeling I have done well in life. I want to live in the house of my choice in an area that will give my family peace and pleasure."

A final way of considering goals is as "have-to" goals and the "want-to" goals. "Have-to" goals are common in the workplace, where people often have goals or targets imposed on them. They would be far more committed to those goals if they themselves had set them. When you establish your own goals in this way it is less likely that other people when you set your own goals, you will be seen as motivated and eager to make things happen, rather than as waiting around watching things

Setting goals and objectives

happen or, even worse, wondering what on earth did happen. Such an attitude demonstrates that you have the necessary initiative to take on more responsibility and to move up the ladder within your company.

Setting goals and objectives is the way to give yourself and your life direction. Without them, you will lack motivation, and your levels of achievement will certainly be lower than your potential. Goals can be likened to signposts on a road that tell you you are on the right road and are making progress towards your destination. Without them, you would be like an aimless traveler, taking one wrong turn after another.

Without goals, it is impossible to prioritize your tasks, as you cannot determine which tasks are more important and in what order they should be done. Maybe you haven't set any long-term goals in your life. This is often due to lack of guidance and understanding of the importance of having goals direct your course in life. It may also be that some of the reasons below have applied to you up to now:

You may think you need a lot of luck to achieve success in life. Luck has been defined as the following:

L - laboring
U - under
C - controlled
K - knowledge

When you consider luck in this way, you realize that we can, to a considerable degree, control what happens to us. A famous golfer was quoted as saying: "The more I practice, the luckier I get." Similarly, the more disciplined you are in setting yourself some really meaningful goals, the luckier you will become. It is easy to look at people who are successful and think, "Oh, they are lucky," rather then recognizing that they made their own luck through sheer hard work.

- "I've done pretty well in my life so far without setting any goals, so why do I need them now?"
- "I know what I want, it's all in my head so I really don't need to write it down."
- "I will feel like a failure if I set goals and then don't achieve them."
- "Setting goals and achieving them will mean people will expect even more of me."
- "I like to be spontaneous in life, and I think setting clear goals takes that away."

- "I just want so much from life, I don't know where to begin with my goals."

Setting goals and writing them down is the best way to motivate yourself and develop your own potential. Goals can be short-term, medium-term, and long-term. In any case, they will provide a framework for you to determine what is important and to prioritize tasks within the time available.

The next stage is to ask yourself: "What actions am I taking to make these goals a reality?" If the answer is little or none, ask yourself what changes you need to make in order to realize your objectives. Then, you can look back on your life in later years and say, "Yes, I did it," rather than, "I wish I'd done it."

Action plans

An action plan should incorporate all the "why," "what," and "how" goals, as well as the more detailed steps, in order to make and monitor progress. It is not only that we take some action that is important, it is also that we enable ourselves to monitor our progress as we go along. This can also have the effect of making us feel good about ourselves. There is a saying that is relevant here: "A journey of a thousand miles starts with a single step." It's just a case of how many "single steps" or bite-size chunks are needed to complete the whole project. Another saying, "Getting started is half done," recognizes that getting started is very often the most difficult part.

Action plan	
Goal:	**Type:**
Reason or Rationale	
1	4
2	5
3	6
Major benefit to me	**to others**
Barriers	**Solutions**
1	
2	
3	
4	
5	
6	
7	

Action plan					
Action stepping stones	complete date	date achieved	time spent	result achieved	reward achieved
1					
2					
3					
4					
5					
Overall target date:					
Positive self-talk 1:					
Positive self-talk 2:					
The commitment to myself:					

Action plans

A sample action plan on a common theme: weight loss!

Action plan		
Goal: To weigh 140 lbs	**Type:**	Medium-term, affecting physical health
Why wanted		
1 To look good and feel better	5 To feel more comfortable in clothing	
2 To be healthier and energetic	6	
3 To feel more confident	7	
4 To be able to take a more active part in sports	8	
Major benifit to me It will increase my confidence and belief in myself.	**To others** They will enjoy being with someone with greater self-esteem.	
Barriers	**Solutions**	
1 I am 15 lbs overweight.	Count calories, and follow a plan.	
2 I am very busy – no time to plan food intake.	Plan intermediate goals: calorie intake and short exercise time.	
3 Food is one of my reasons to live.	Reward myself for cutting down.	
4 I don't enjoy exercising.	Do the exercises I do enjoy – walking and cycling.	
5 I enjoy eating out (don't have to cook).	Eat out less, and ask others for support.	

Action plan					
Action stepping stones Present weight 155 lbs	**complete date**	**date achieved**	**hours taken**	**result achieved**	**reward achieved**
1 Lose 3 lbs. Exercise, walk, cycle – 10 minutes, 3 times per week.	Feb 1	Jan 28	2 hrs	Very good	Yes
2 Lose 3 more lbs. Maintain agreed calorie intake.	Mar 1	Mar 3	2.5 hrs	Good	Yes
3 Lose 3 more lbs. Increase exercise to 4 times per week.	Apr 1	Apr 1	2.7 hrs	Good	Yes
4 Lose 3 more lbs. Increase exercise to 4 times per week -15 mins each session.	May 1	May 8	4 hrs	Fair	Yes
5 Lose 3 more lbs. Continue to exercise 4 times per week for 20 minutes each session.	Jun 1	May 31	5.3 hrs	Very good	Yes
Feel good, clothes fit well & have more energy					
Overall target date: July 1	May need to readjust, depending on progress				
Positive self talk 1: My weight is now 140 lbs	**Positive self talk 2:** I am enjoying more energy and feel better.				
The commitment to myself: I am committed to following this plan and will adjust my lifestyle to achieve this goal.	Date January 1 Signature K. Jones				

Use more than one plan

The above example gives you a good template for developing your own action plans. You could have several action plans covering career, family, and hobbies. Initially, however, it would be best to concentrate on one area of your life at a time. Otherwise, you could feel demotivated before you even start. Once you start to achieve some success in that area, you will be spurred on to create action plans for other goals.

Preparing a time log

You have probably experienced days when you have gone home from work and thought, "I feel as if I have achieved nothing today." Preparing a time log will give you valuable information as to why you sometimes feel this way.

In order to be aware of how time can just "disappear," a time log over a period of at least one week. It will show you when you are interrupted and what type of interruption it is. Is it the telephone? Is it people in the office? Is it customers? You will be able to use your time log to identify this kind of information, and that will help you to manage the interruptions. It may also reveal the quieter times of the day, when you could take some time to do other tasks that are part of your job.

PERSONAL TIME LOG		Date	Day
To be completed every 15 minutes			

Time	Use	Time	Use
8:00 a.m.		10:45	
8:15		11:00	
8:30		11:15	
8:45		11:30	
9:00		11:45	
9:15		12:00	
9:30		12:15	
9:45		12:30	
10:00		12:45	
10:15		1:00 p.m.	
10:30		1:15	

The following example of a time log is divided into 15-minute sections. The idea is that you record what happens every 15 minutes throughout the day, and into the evening as well, if you want to make better use of your leisure time. Completing this exercise will provide you with some real help in making the changes you need – and want – in your life. When you have factual information, you have data with which to work. But when you have only vague feelings about wasted time, it's difficult to identify what changes should be made. Please continue your record for the evening on another sheet.

Time	Use	Time	Use
1:30		4:00	
1:45		4:15	
2:00		4:30	
2:15		4:45	
2:30		5:00	
2:45		5:15	
3:00		5:30	
3:15		5:45	
3:30		6:00	
3:45		6:15	

Prioritizing tasks

From your action plans, you will have identified the different tasks you need to carry out on a daily basis. The next stage is to decide what priority each task has. This will be determined by a number of factors, including whether they are short-term, medium-term, or long-term goals. You will need to allocate time each day for dealing with the reactive tasks, as well as proactive and maintenance tasks, as these are inevitable.

However, you can often reduce the length of time you spend on some of these tasks, once you have recognized how much time you currently spend on reactive tasks.

There are some other important factors that determine the priority various tasks have, that is to say, how important and how urgent are they?

Importance and urgency

Consider some of the tasks in your working day. Ask yourself how important and urgent they are.

Rate the tasks according to their priority on the corresponding charts.

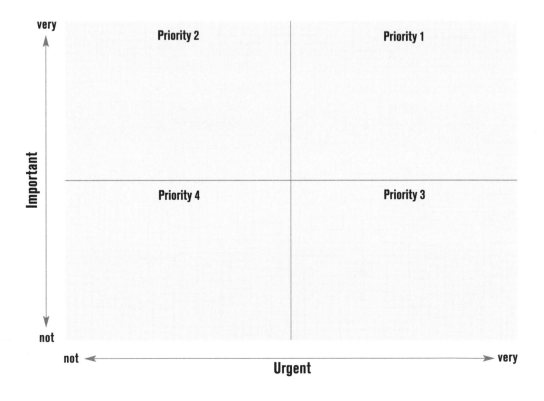

The tasks can be broken down into five categories:
- **Important and urgent**
- **Important, not urgent**
- **Urgent, not important**
- **Busy work**
- **Wasted time**

Let's look at each of these in turn:

Important and urgent – Priority 1

These are the tasks that have to be done immediately or in the very near future.

Important, not urgent – Priority 2

These tasks can be done either now or later. However, they are tasks that will significantly affect the completion of projects, and they will become Priority 1 in a short period of time.

Urgent, not important – Priority 3

These are unimportant tasks that require immediate action, such as attending a low-level meeting or making a routine phone call.

Busy work – Priority 4

These are the tasks that are neither important nor urgent. We sometimes use them to convince ourselves that we are very busy, when we may be just moving paper around the desk. Generally, these are tasks you should not make part of your action plan.

Wasted time

These are the things we engage in that do not achieve anything at all; for example, excessive socializing at work with colleagues or on the telephone. Please note the word "excessive:" An element of social chat is useful in building relationships with colleagues, customers, and suppliers. However, excessive socializing prevents you from getting on with other, more important tasks.

You can rate degrees of both urgency and importance using the box below as a guide:

Importance
1 = **Crucial**
   Must be finished
2 = **Important**
   Will cause a problem if not completed
3 = **Unimportant**
   No serious repercussions if not completed

Urgency
1 = **High**
   Essential that it is done today
2 = **Medium**
   Essential that it is finished this week
3 = **Low**
   A job to be fitted in any time

Prioritizing tasks or Assigning Priorities

	Task	Priority	Start date	Finish date	Delegate?	Progress review
1						
2						
3						
4						
5						
6						
7						
8						
9						
10						

"To-Do" lists

Your prioritized tasks can be assembled into a useful "To-do" list, as shown above.

There will sometimes be more than one Priority 1 task on your list. Then you will need to rank under those. Do the more complicated ones first in your prime time, when you are most alert. This will add to your confidence, make you feel good, and motivate you to tackle the other jobs. It is also important to give yourself short breaks, particularly when undertaking a very complicated task, so that you can come back to it feeling refreshed. It is generally recognized that 45 minutes is the maximum time span for high-concentration levels. Beyond that your ability to keep your mind on the job starts to waver. A 10-minute break from a high-priority task, during which you do some Prioritiy 3 chores, such as making phone calls or dictating a letter, provides a mental break.

A "To-Do" list takes the various items in your Action Plan and divides them into the tasks you will do on a daily basis.

Here is an example of what a typical list could look like:

To Do Today (Date:)	
8:00	**Must Do** **Customer meetings**
9:00 Office procedures – Distribute mail. Make phone calls.	Office procedures - mail Letters
10:00 Meet with customer.	Attend meeting.
11:00 Do word processing letters.	
12:00 Meet with supervisor.	**Should Do** **Marketing plan**
13:00 Lunch	Business-development calls
14:00 Marketing – Plan & prepare direct mail.	Forward planning
15:00 Meet with customer.	**Could Do** **Talk to staff about marketing plans.**
16:00 Make phone calls. Business development – develop list of contacts.	
17:00 Plan for tomorrow.	
18:00 Go to the gym.	

Paper management

A specific aspect of managing time is managing the paper on your desk (and at home). Your objective should be to handle each piece of paper only once. If you tend to shuffle papers around your desk, this objective will be particularly important for you. Avoid allowing stacks of paper to clutter up your desk; your desk is a working area, not a storage space.

Be disciplined with your paperwork. Deal with it immediately by choosing one of these four options:

- Act on it immediately.
- Pass it on to someone else.
- File it.
- Put it in the wastepaper basket.

Let's take a look at these options in more detail.

Action it immediately

Read it, reply to it, or put it in a planner if it will require action in the future. Enter it in a computer or in a conventional planner.

Passing it onto someone else

This is done if you need information before you can deal with the item. It is important to keep track so that you can meet your own deadlines. You will need to make a note in your planning system on the date you want a reply and on the

item, itself. In other words, clearly communicate what you want to happen and by when.

File it

If you are going to file the piece of paper, have a file basket and a regular time marked in your planner for doing the filing, so that this routine task does not become a choice.

The regularity with which you do the filing will depend on how quickly your paperwork accumulates. It may be something you need to schedule daily or weekly, depending on the volume generated.

Put it in the wastepaper basket

Finally, it is important to recognize that much of the paper that lands on your desk is not relevant to you. Make sure you put as much as possible in the wastepaper basket. Don't be tempted to keep it "just in case." Transcribe any information you need; then throw it away.

Use your planner to allocate time once a month to review your files. Be ruthless in throwing out any paperwork you do not need. Ask yourself: "Have I referred to this in the last month?" If the answer is "no," then you can afford to dispose of it. If you do allow papers to pile up, filing them becomes a mammoth task leading to that old enemy, procrastination.

The use of the telephone

Here is a piece of technology that, if not managed properly, can easily become a time waster. Use your time log to analyze how much time you spend on calls, both incoming and outgoing. Ask yourself whether you could have spent less time on your telephone calls and, if so, how.

Some telephone habits that can waste time are:

- Too much social chat
- Not having paper and pens ready for writing down messages
- Not preparing what you want to say
- Not giving precise answers
- Having to answer all incoming calls
- Having to deal with "difficult" people
- Taking calls when you are in the middle of a high-priority project
- Not listening properly
- Not knowing how to deal with an answering machine

Here are some principles for saving time on the telephone. These are split into two groups, one for incoming calls and one for outgoing calls. Some of the principles apply to both groups.

Incoming calls

- Keep your social chat to a minimum.
- Make answers brief and to the point.
- Actively listen to what the caller is saying; close your mind off from whatever you were doing, and focus completely on the person with whom you are talking. This takes some practice if you are easily distracted.
- If possible, delegate the task of answering the phone to a colleague. If telephone interruptions are a major problem when you are doing high-priority tasks, consider installing an answering machine or voice mail.
- If there is someone who can take calls for you, consider refusing to take calls at certain times of the day. Make sure the message-taker gets an idea of why the caller wants to speak to you.
- Check your understanding of what the caller has said by summarizing the content of the discussion.
- Always have pen and paper nearby for writing down messages. A preprinted pad for taking messages, especially if you take them for other people, is ideal.
- Be the last person to put the phone down. There are times when the caller remembers something they wanted to say just as you are putting the phone down. If you wait until they put it down, then you can be confident that they have finished.

The use of the telephone

- Thank the person for calling you.
- If you say you are going to call back, make sure you do so, and within an agreed timeframe. There is nothing worse than saying you will call someone back and then not doing so. Three hours later, they may be wasting time, still waiting for the call – a familiar situation for all of us!

OUTGOING CALLS

- Be prepared. Plan what you want to say and what you want the outcome to be.
- When you make the calls, you are at an advantage psychologically because you are interrupting the other person's work schedule at a time that suits you.
- Plan the message you will leave if you are greeted by an answering machine. Make it short, simple, and to the point.
- If you have to make a call that you are not looking forward to, visualize a positive outcome by running the situation through your mind beforehand; and increase your feeling of authority by standing up. Being upright enables you to breathe more easily, which has a direct effect on how you speak. It also permits you to take some deep breaths to calm you down when you are dealing with a difficult person.
- Listen actively. Listen to the tone of voice, as well as the words. This will give you clues to the emotional state of the other person.
- Take notes of any actions you promise to carry out for the person.
- Be the last person to put the phone down so that you can be sure that the other person has said everything he or she wanted to say.

GENERAL PRINCIPLES FOR THE USE OF THE TELEPHONE IN THE OFFICE

- Phones should be answered as quickly as possible, preferably within three rings. Make sure everyone understands the importance of answering the phone and that they have sufficient knowledge to answer simple questions in a confident manner. Being able to direct calls to the right department is very important. There is nothing worse than being passed from pillar to post.

- Ensure that there are good procedures in place for taking messages and passing them on to the relevant person. At the very least, write down the caller's name, organization, telephone number and a good time to call back.

- If you have to answer a phone when you are eating, drinking, or smoking, make sure this is not obvious. Stop what you are doing as quickly as possible, and listen actively.

- Put the phone on hold if you need to speak to someone else. The caller does not need to hear your attempt to answer his or her question.

- If you cannot answer a question, and there is no one around to ask, tell the caller that you will call back with the information. Be sure to do what you have promised.

Attending and running meetings

A meeting is another classic opportunity for time-wasting. People who don't stick to the point or pursue pointless arguments; unprepared participants; meeting leaders who lose control of the proceedings; and meetings held for the sake of having a meeting, rather than because they are necessary, are just a few of the problems that plague meetings. How often do people come away from a meeting saying, "That was a waste of time." That is not the reaction to a well-run meeting.

Here are some guidelines to ensure that meetings are not a waste of time. Do you or your organization hold meetings for the sake of it? Is it a question of, "Oh, it's Tuesday, so we have the planning meeting?" Very often

THE "TO-DO" LIST FOR A GOOD MEETING

- Have specific goals clearly spelled out.
- Give everyone who attends the opportunity to contribute to the agenda.
- Prepare a typed agenda, with allotted time for each topic according to its priority, and circulate it to everyone before the meeting so that they can prepare their comments.
- Be sure the people you invite have a reason to be there.
- Appoint a chairperson to direct the meeting, a secretary to take the minutes, and a timekeeper to keep things on track.
- Vary your start times. By doing something different – setting a time to start a meeting at 10:10, for example – you convey the message that you are serious. People will be there on time.
- Be punctual; show your commitment to the meeting by arriving before the start time.
- Have an agreed finishing time, and be sure you adhere to it.
- Adopt a set of ground rules by which everyone must abide. The ground rules could include listening attentively, not interrupting other people, being punctual, showing respect to everyone else, and being constructive when challenging people's ideas.

organisations get into the habit of holding meetings and never question why the meeting is being held. One way to focus people's minds on the relevance of meetings is to calculate the cost of a meeting. This can be done quite easily by taking the hourly rate of each person who attends and multiplying it by the time spent. If 10 people attend a one-hour meeting, that is 10 hours of time. If the average salary is $30 per hour, the cost of the meeting is $300. Has this meeting produced savings of more than $300 or ideas that will generate more than $300 in extra profit? If not, it is important to ask whether this particular meeting should be held in future or if there are more effective ways of communicating the same information.

THE "TO-DO" LIST FOR A GOOD MEETING

- In some meetings an article is passed around, such as a book, and only the person holding that article may talk. This helps to maintain discipline and time-keeping.
- Keep people's minds focused on the meeting by summarizing what has been decided so far.
- Consider asking each participant to deal with a particular item and to speak for a set time, perhaps five minutes. This has the advantage of getting everyone involved. Stick to the schedule to keep the discussion moving.
- Be focused on the issues. Personal attacks on other people are never constructive. The person under attack may become defensive, and the meeting can very quickly degenerate, becoming chaotic and a waste of time.
- Circulate the minutes soon after the meeting.
- Ensure that the minutes show what actions are to be taken and by whom.
- Put any items that involve you in your planner, and make sure that you move these tasks forward before the next meeting.

Delegation

Delegation is one of those time-management skills that is often not carried out particularly well. This is because many people do not understand the difference between delegating a task and abandoning responsibility for it. Others have a fear of delegation, falling into the trap of thinking that it is quicker and easier to do everything themselves. However, the more tasks you can delegate to other people, the easier it will make your own life. In the event of a crisis, there will be more people able to help you deal with it.

Fears about delegation may be based on the desire to be perfect, or on a lack of trust in a junior colleague. Some people believe it gives them more power to hold on to as many tasks as possibile. The fact that part of delegation is to hand over the task, while still retaining responsibility for it, can be very daunting for many people. There are ways of overcoming such fears as you will see in the guidelines for delegation.

The knowledge, experience, and skills of the person to whom you are delegating a task, as well as his or her general motivation, are important. Does this person learn new things quickly or need a lot of guidance? Does he or she frequently take the initiative in new tasks and projects and demonstrate accuracy and discipline in all activities? All of these attributes will make you more confident about delegating a task to this colleague. However, of equal significance to whether they do a good job within the required time limit is the way in which you delegate the task. These guidelines will help you to delegate effectively:

- **Communicate clearly what action is required.** Poor communication increases the risk of mistakes. The person may make false assumptions and incorrect judgements, which could lead to unfortunate results.
- **Check for understanding by using open questions**. Don't ask, "Are you OK?" or "Do you understand?" If the person doesn't understand, he or she may be reluctant to admit it. Open questions start with words such as who, why, what, when, where, how. Beginning a question with one of these words will ensure that the answer must go beyond a simple "yes" or "no."

- **Consider the existing workload.** Are there already a number of high-priority tasks to complete?
- **Is additional information needed?** If so, make sure it is provided, and consider what training and help could be a help in carrying out the task.
- **Support the person to whom you delegate.** This is especially important for someone who learns slowly and needs confidence building. Make it clear that you are available if you are needed. If you can't be available, find someone who can, and make sure that both parties are aware of each other. If the task you have delegated means the person has to work with other people, introduce everyone properly.
- **Give encouragement.** Show that you have confidence in the person to do a good job, and say so. Refer to another time when he or she did a good job for you or a colleague.
- **Monitor progress.** It is important to get the balance right. Monitor too closely, and it will seem that you are constantly checking to see if progress is being made. This is not a confidence builder. Monitor too little, and the person will feel abandoned. This is not delegation; it is more like abdication. Establish beforehand what feedback you want and at what intervals. In that way, you will both have a clear understanding of what is happening. Then hand over the job, and step aside. Don't monitor progress except at the established times.

REMEMBER THE BENEFITS OF DELEGATION. IT WILL:

- Free up your own time to do more complex tasks
- Test out a bright person to see how well he or she performs
- Provide opportunities for an assistant or direct report to gain useful experience for the future

Frameworks for gathering information and ideas

Brainstorming is a way of developing new ideas. It can be more productive than writing ideas on paper in a linear format because it frees your thinking power from the straitjacket of mere logic.

When we use a linear approach to note-taking, we are using only the left side of the brain – the side that deals with logic, lists, lines, words, numbers, and the ordering of information.

We are encouraged to use this side of the brain at school because it is thought to be the most important.

The right side of the brain deals with the more creative aspects of processing and generating information – color, rhythm, music, imagination, and daydreaming. Were you ever chastised by your parents or teachers for daydreaming? And do you feel guilty now if you catch yourself doing it? Well, here's the good news: we need to use both sides of our brains in order to maximize our potential, and daydreaming plays an important role in that process. The more activities we can involve ourselves in that use both sides

of our brains, the more effective we will be in our jobs and in our lives.

In the 1950s it was thought that people used about 50 percent of their brainpower, but it is now known that the actual percentage is far less. Research has shown that we use only about one percent of our potential brainpower. Just imagine the amount of creativity we fail to exploit.

Brainstorming is way to increase this percentage and to get as many ideas as possible from a group of people. It is important that initially no judgement is made on the ideas. In fact, the more bizarre they become, the better. No ideas should not be rejected at this stage of the process, as this will limit our association, which is an important part of the process. More ideas spring from those already given, enabling you to build up as many options as possible. Once the list appears to be exhausted, you can then apply criteria to all the suggestions given to enable you to have various ways of solving a problem or moving a project forward.

Mind Mapping

A brainstorming technique that was developed by Tony Buzan is "Mind Mapping." This links both sides of the brain together to enable you to make associations, something you have a natural ability to do. It is just that you have probably never had it explained to you! This linking process combines the logic of the left brain with the creativity of the right brain, resulting in the generation of more ideas, more quickly.

The technique involves using paper in an unconventional way. You place a symbol in the middle of a page to represent whatever it is you want to create ideas about in order to develop different options. Then you take offshoots from that central image as ideas come into your mind that relate to your main topic. You will find that you have more ideas put down on paper than if you used the conventional list-style format. The more color and symbols you use to give the Mind Map life, the more effective it will be.

A Mind Map will help you in many areas, including planning, gathering information, solving problems, or deciding on a plan of action. Alternatively, it can be used for taking minutes of meetings or summarising the contents of an article. Mind mapping permits you to have the key points on only one sheet of paper, making it more likely that you will use the information.

Below is a very basic Mind Map on generating ideas for different rewards you can give yourself as you succeed in your various stages of time management.

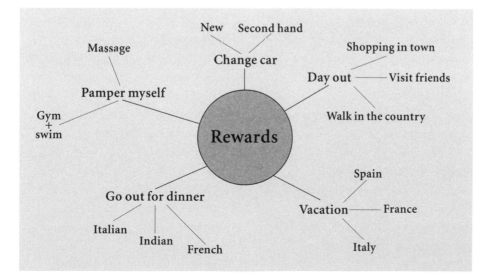

Personal development

Personal development has two aspects – change and learning. The change is very personal because it is about changing yourself. The learning is finding out about yourself – how you do things now and what could be more effective in the future. One of the strongest barriers to overcome will almost certainly be that you have self-limiting beliefs about yourself. These can be changed through positive affirmations, visualization, and a determination to succeed. The question to ask yourself here is: "Am I prepared to invest some time in myself in order to live a more balanced lifestyle by using new time-management principles?"

Personal-development plans are designed to help you to grow and develop your skills and realize your potential through both conscious and unconscious learning. Usually included are elements of planned study, such as working through this book, as well as experience, which is frequently supported by someone who acts as a coach. This is where a mentor – either within your organization, or outside of it – is particularly useful. If you have the opportunity to be part of a mentoring relationship seize the opportunity with great enthusiasm. Using someone else's experience to help you is extremely beneficial.

Everyone likes encouragement, whether it is help from friends, colleagues, a boss, or someone who we see as a good role model.

Your own responsibility

One of the many benefits of a personal development plan is that you take the primary responsibility for what you learn. You choose what you learn, when to do it, and what suits you. You also decide when to complete one topic and move onto something else. As it is a form of self-development, what you choose to learn is likely to affect the "whole person," as a manager at work, as a parent at home, and as a member of the community.

To gain the maximum benefit from a development plan, you need to take responsibility for your own choices about what you want to learn. A great help to this process is receiving the insight, feedback, and ideas of others. Both honest feedback and constructive criticism are needed to overcome your blocks and blind spots.

If you have ever been videotaped as part of a training program, you will understand how much you can learn from seeing yourself as others see you. For many people, it is not a particularly comfortable experience initially. However, it is a very powerful learning tool.

Why prepare a personal development plan?

The reason for writing a personal development plan is usually because you are dissatisfied with your present situation – in this case, not enough time to do all the things you want to do. You also want to understand why and how you should move forward. You have four choices when you are dissatisfied with a situation:

- Put up with the situation.
- Leave it.
- Get others to change.
- Change yourself.

The last option is the most effective and clearly shows that you are taking responsibility for your actions.

The other aspect of managing others is that it often reveals that you are not very good at managing yourself. In order to be effcctive manager, it is imperative that you manage yourself well. This book will help you in one of the important areas of self-management, that of managing your time in a more effective way.

Good self-management should enable you to have a good balance in the following areas:

Action : Relaxation
Work : Home
Head : Heart
Doing : Being

Many managers have never had any formal training and do not realize the benefit of taking the time to reflect on their own strengths and weaknesses. In particular, they do not understand the process of learning and how they learn best as individuals. There is a model of the learning process, which explains all the stages you need to undertake in order to have a complete learning experience. This are shown below.

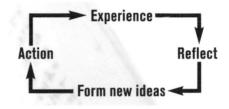

You can dip into this learning cycle at any point. What is important is that you go through every stage. So, if you have some new ideas as a result of reading this book, you would put them into action and gain some experience in how well they work. Finally, you would take time to think about how well the new ideas worked. To go through each process will enhance your ability to learn, rather than interfering with it.

Another benefit of your own personal development plan is that you are learning because you want to, rather than at someone else's insistence. It is also important to recognize that "doing" needs much more commitment than "saying."

Personal development

Remember, for your continuing development, set yourself challenging, yet realistic, goals. When they have been accomplished, build on that success, and set new goals. Make a commitment to making those changes you have identified for yourself – those you want and choose in order to improve your lifestyle. Be bold. Take that first step in a journey that may appear, at this moment, to be a very long one.

You will have to overcome your internal conditioning, as your subconscious mind will initially resist any changes you want to make. It will be thinking that the old way was OK, so why do you need to change? The answer is quite simple: If you want different results, you need to make some changes in the way you work and, in particular, how you manage your time. There is a saying that brings this message home: "Insanity is... doing the same old things and expecting different results." Remember, this is a commitment to you, for you. The only person to reap the benefits will be you, though possibly your family as well, if you get to spend more time with them.

Stages to personal development

Here are the stages to work through:

- Begin with a desire to change and learn.
- Self-diagnosis: you make the decisions, and you make the choices about what to do. This can be based on feedback you have received from others.
- Set goals: what do you want to be different, or what would your ideal situation look like?
- Design a learning program.
- Decide what actions you will take.
- Regularly review the outcomes, preferably with another person.

- Look at the resources you will need, including people, books and research materials, time, and money.
- Seek encouragement from other people.
- Develop perseverance and persistence.

All of this will help your development as a self-starter who takes the initiative – a quality that is highly valued in many organizations today. It enables you to have flexibility and adaptability. Both qualities are vital for success.

Making the changes happen

Below are the actions you will need to take in order to make successful changes in your life. This saying may help you along the way: "Invest one percent of each day's working time in yourself, and the other 99 per cent will benefit." The following are the necessary actions:

- **Build confidence.** When you start new tasks, remember the times when you have been successful in the past. Accept negative feelings as part of the process of change. Confidence is the ability to lift yourself above those feelings, past mistakes and failures.

- **Develop self-belief in an active way, by developing yourself.** Start with small steps and build from there. This includes overcoming frustration and approaching tasks with enthusiasm.

- **Develop new goals.** This helps overcomes frustration.

- **Concentrate on one task at a time** Live in the present, not in the past or the future.

- **Develop a sense of understanding.** Be gentle with yourself and others. Show an interest in others, and compliment them genuinely. Make others feel important; excessive criticism is damaging to their egos.

- **Focus on communication skills and rapport.** Understand that the way you think and feel will have an impact on how you communicate with others. The way you act as a result of your experiences will be different from the way other people act. You will have to make allowances and ask questions to understand their point of view.

- **Give yourself praise for the jobs you do well.**

- **Develop a major, absorbing obsession.** Whatever we want in life is worth the effort required. Become completely absorbed with your plan for life, and you will find that totally unexpected doors open up for you.

- **Treat difficulties as opportunities to learn.** These are often indicators and openings to guide you in the right direction.

- **Develop persistence.** Confidence and belief grows when you keep going in difficult circumstances.

- **Use affirmations to become the way you want to be.** "My persistence will allow me to find the means to do this job."

- **Develop an expectant, winning attitude.** What we expect in life usually becomes reality, so expect the best for yourself.

- **Develop a win-win attitude.** Help others to win and succeed, and you will be rewarded with success yourself. You must also accept 100 percent responsibility for yourself.

Personal development

- Recognize that it is the way you react to situations that leads to problems, not the situations themselves.

- **Look for solutions.** Do not blame others when things go wrong. Being responsible means looking forward; blame looks backward.

- **Develop the courage to do what it takes!** Courage and responsibility go together. Fear can be conquered by "doing it anyway." Being willing to do something usually creates the courage to do it.

- **Develop a happy state of mind.** You must make good things happen. If you expect external things to make you happy, you will be disappointed. Share your happiness with others. There is nothing as uplifting at work and in your life away from the office as being around a happy person.

- **Replace negative thoughts with positive thoughts.** Develop "I can" thinking, rather than "I can't" thinking.

Remember FEAR is:

F- False
E - Evidence
A - Appearing
R - Real

Conclusion

All of these qualities are necessary to obtain success in life. Success is about achieving the goals you set for yourself, not comparing yourself and what you have achieved with someone else, such as your colleagues, bosses, or neighbors. Comparisons with other people will only engender a feeling of dissatisfaction, which is totally non-productive. Many people fall into this trap. Work hard to keep yourself free from doing so.

To bring this section to a conclusion, on the next page is an example of a personal development plan that you can use to establish your own plan. Use all the information in this section on development. It will help you gain a greater understanding of yourself, how you work, your current level of skills, and the areas that would benefit from further work – not just your time management skills, but all your management skills.

Personal Development Plan

PERSONAL/PRIVATE OBJECTIVES (What do I want to achieve in the next year / 5 years)	GAP IN KNOWLEDGE / SKILLS (What gaps are there in my skills / knowledge that prevent me from achieving this at present?)
1. 2. 3.	

DEVELOPMENT PLAN (What training / development will I undertake in order to bridge this gap?)	DEVELOPMENT OBJECTIVES (What will I be able to do as a result of completing the training / development?)
1. 2.	1. 2. 3. 4. 1. 2. 3. 4.

WHO WILL I ASK TO BE MY MENTOR / COACH?	WHAT SUPPORT DO I WANT FROM THEM?

Recognizing what you have learned

You have traveled a long way through this book and been exposed to many new ideas, as well as retrieved others that had been consigned to your subconscious. It is time to implement all of those ideas in order to become a more effective time manager.

Remember, for your continuing development, set yourself challenging but realistic goals. When you have accomplished them, build on that success by setting new goals. You have come a long way, but success is a journey, not a desitnation.

Learning review 1

What have been the major lessons you have learned from reading this book? Prioritize your list in order to help you achieve your goals. Prepare an action plan that incorporates these learning points and decide on a realistic time frame in which to implement them.
What benefits are there for you in the:
a) short term
b) medium term
c) long term
What benefits are there for others in your life?
a) family
b) friends
c) colleagues
d) your boss
e) your company

Learning Review 2

1. When setting goals for yourself, why is it important to ensure they are all SMART goals?

2. Using your time logs compiled over the next week, what percentage of your time will be spent on each type of task – proactive, reactive, and maintenance?

3. Is your time allocation in proportion to the significance of your tasks?

4. What actions will you take to make changes to ensure that your time is spent on the areas that produce results?

Learning review 3
Self-discipline

Self-discipline is an important aspect of time management. It may seem easier to let others to direct us and to blame them when our lives don't work out the way we want them to; but, in the long run, we will feel more in control of our own lives if we learn to take responsibility for the things we do.

The entire process of improving your time-management skills requires self-discipline. The obvious place to start is to review and decide on your "WHY," "WHAT," and "HOW" goals. From there, you will want to be sure that these goals fulfilled the SMART criteria before devizing your action plan.

A good question to ask about your self-discipline, whether you are at work or at home, is the following: "Is what I am doing right now helping me to achieve my goals?"

When you are faced with a large task or project to complete, there are times when you will think: "I really don't know where to start." This is where your action plan will help you, to break down the whole task into smaller chunks in a steady, disciplined way. This discipline in taking the time – probably, in most cases, no more than 10 minutes – to break the task down and analyze it, is essential to effective time management. The result is that you will feel much more in control of your job, and you will also earn a reputation as someone who is reliable.

A final point on discipline – your daily "To-do" list ideally should be prepared last thing before leaving work so that when you come in first thing in the morning, your day is already planned. If you leave planning until the morning, the danger is that other events will sidetrack you and, before you know where you are, it will be mid-morning and you will not have done any top-priority work.

4

Maintaining new skills
Learning styles
Developing the skill in others

Overcoming learning blockages
Conclusions

Ways of maintaining new skills

There is only one way to stay better anything and that is to practice, practice, practice. Maintaining the self-discipline of your new found time-management principles will be of the utmost importance. On the other hand, if you slip back some days, don't be too hard on yourself. Feelings of self-recrimination are not productive in any way and will not contribute to your overall desire to keep improving.

If you find you are slipping backward regularly, ask yourself why it is happening. If the answer is that you are too busy to plan and organize your time, what is that telling you about yourself?

There are one or two other ideas that may help to throw some light on this issue. Your own individual method of learning new ideas affects your ability to succeed. In order to have a complete learning process, you need to understand all the different ways there are of learning. These fall into four categories:

People differ in where their strengths and weaknesses are. They can feel uncomfortable and discouraged when their weaker skills are required. For example, some people love doing new things and do not think twice about the consequences. For them, the learning is in the doing and the excitement of something new. But this type of learner may not enjoy thinking about the experience or forming ideas about it, so a lot of the potential learning is lost.

There are others who do not like to take any action on a problem until they have read a lot of books about it. For example, they will read several manuals before using a new computer. When they have all the facts and possible information, only then will they switch on the machine. This type of learner will miss out on the kind of learning that is derived from being spontaneous and instinctive.

In order to help you identify your strengths – and whether you have a combination of two, three, or all four behavior types – here are some descriptions of the "likes" and "dislikes" of each category.

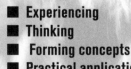

- ■ Experiencing
- ■ Thinking
- ■ Forming concepts
- ■ Practical application

Learning preferences

Consider the "likes" and "dislikes" of each style of learning, and work out the composition of your own learning skills. Once you have identified that, consider how it affects your ability to put all the new ideas you have learned from this book into practice. Depending on what you find out about yourself, it could help you overcome your reluctance to develop your time-management skills over the coming months.

THE EXPERIENCER	
"LIKES"	"DISLIKES"
New experiences, challenges, opportunities	Non-active roles, listening
Doing things in the "here and now"	Not being involved
Excitement, drama, crisis	Having to analyze information
Being seen, a high profile	Lots of theory
In at the deep end – overcoming difficulties	Doing the same old things
Being with people	Working alone
Giving it a try	Precise instructions with no flexibility
Generating ideas without constraints	Thinking before, evaluating after

Learning preferences

THE PRACTICAL PERSON	
"LIKES"	**"DISLIKES"**
Linking theory to practical situations	Being unable to see any immediate practical benefit or relevance
Any practical techniques	Lots of theory and principles with no reality about them
To give and receive useful feedback	Lack of guidelines for carrying out tasks
Being with a good and effective role model	Not making progress, feeling of going round and round
Ideas that apply to the job at hand	Petty obstacles preventing things happening
Opportunities to use new ideas	Lack of reward for using new ideas
Working with "real" problems	Using practical issues to prepare action plans that will have a positive outcome

THE THINKER	
"LIKES"	**"DISLIKES"**
Thinking, observing, contemplating	Being forced into a high-profile position
Standing back, listening, watching	Taking action without any pre-planning
Gathering information, investigating in depth	Having to draw a conclusion based on limited information
Opportunity to reflect on learning	Specific instructions on how to carry out a task
Opportunity to discuss and exchange views on a problem	Having to take short cuts or do a "superficial" job
Time for considered analysis of reports and data	Being under time pressures, rushing from one job to another

THE CONCEPTS PERSON	
"LIKES"	**"DISLIKES"**
Systems, models, concepts, theories	Tasks with no apparent purpose
Methodical exploration of ideas, tasks, problems	Being involved in any emotional situations
Questioning methods, assumptions, and logic	Activities with no structure
Mastering intellectually complex tasks	Taking action without it being based on solid principles
To be clear on the purpose of a task	To be faced with a lot of options, none of which has been thought through
To be able to analyze the likely success or failure of a task	Subjects that appear to have no depth or are seen as gimmicks

Conclusion

Depending on your preference, the way in which you learn will have an impact on how easy it is to change some of your existing habits. Most people are a combination of all four categories, with higher preferences for one or two of the styles.

If your learning preference leans towards the practical, you will want to see some direct benefits before deciding to make some changes to the way you currently manage your time. If you are someone who likes to spend time thinking about what you will do differently, the format of this book will be ideally suited to your learning preference. If, on the other hand, you prefer to experience directly, having to complete questionnaires and To-Do lists will appear to be a real chore.

If you like dealing with concepts and ideas, then the style of this book should have considerable appeal for you. It will enable you to experiment with the different principles and monitor the results.

Overcoming learning blocks

Blocks to "Experiencing"

- Making mistakes and a fear of failure
- Being ridiculed
- Fear of unfamiliar situations
- Needing to think everything through
- Lack of self-confidence
- Regarding life as very serious

Ways to overcome these blocks

- Choose something that you have not done before, and do it once a week, e.g. read a different newspaper, or do something spontaneous one evening.
- Introduce yourself to people you do not know at a party or meeting.
- Change the activity you are doing at work every half an hour every few days, so it breaks your usual routine.
- Make yourself more visible. Volunteer to get involved in different activities such as running a meeting or giving a presentation.
- Practise thinking on your feet. Get a group of people together where each has to give a five-minute presentation (with no preparation).

Blockages to "Thinking Style"

- Lack of time to plan or think
- Others being impatient for action
- Preferring to keep moving from one activity to another
- Reluctance to listen attentively and analyse what is being said
- Reluctance to make any notes

Ways to overcome these blocks

- Think of a topic that you would like to know more about, and set yourself a goal to research it.
- Think of an issue that occurred at work or at home, and draw up arguments representing both sides of the situation.
- When you are with people who want to go straight into action, intervene by making them think about all the options and consequences of each.
- Make a point of studying other people's behavior and their body language. Meetings are a good place to do this. Also look for people who interrupt each other (who and when and what the disagreements are about).
- Take time each day to write a journal; then decide whether there are any conclusions to be drawn. If so, write them in the journal.
- Take time to review events, such as meetings. Define what went well, what could have gone better, and what you would do differently next time.

Blocks to "Concepts Style"

- Always taking situations at face value
- Preferring to work intuitively
- Disliking structure in life
- Preferring spontaneity

Ways to overcome these blocks

- Spend 30 minutes each day reading a thought-provoking book or article on such topics as philosophy. Alternatively, read a management textbook. Then spend some time summarizing the content.
- Read two newspapers with different viewpoints on the same topic and analyze the differences. When you listen to other people arguing a point, take time to think about any inconsistencies or weaknesses in what they have said. You can do a similar exercise with documents that propose a course of action.
- Make a point of asking probing questions, and don't be satisfied with nonspecific answers. Questions starting with "Why" are usually very probing.

Blocks to "Practical Style"

- Looking for perfect rather than practical solutions to problems
- Thinking that useful tips are gimmicks
- Being easily sidetracked
- Preferring to leave things open-ended
- Feeling that other people's ideas will not work in your situation

Ways to overcome these blocks

- Watch how other people do things and practice those that work well.
- At any discussion or meeting, always have a list of actions you will take as a result of the meeting.
- Look for opportunities to use and experiment with new techniques. If they will have an impact on other people, tell them what you are planning to do first.
- Decide on a practical project to do, such as decorating around the house, becoming familiar with different aspects of a computer, or learning a foreign language.

Conclusion

This section has provided more information about you and the way you learn, which will affect the way you approach tasks, both at work and at home. Having identified the blocks to learning, look closely at the suggestions for overcoming them. These ideas for developing yourself will have benefits in all areas of your life. Many of the ideas will encourage you to take different approaches to existing tasks. You are also likely to find that you take a more open-minded approach, which in itself will have additional benefits, as you will not be bound by past thinking.

As the saying goes, "Our minds are like parachutes; they work best when they are open."

So having looked at this final section and recognised the various blockages that can occur for each learning type, together with some suggestions for overcoming these, you are well placed to set yourself a project on using your learning preferences to help you in your objective to manage your time better. Recognise that everybody has a mixture of learning preferences and it is knowing which ones will help you and which ones will hinder you in your personal development that is the key.

Passing on the learning

The new habits you are committed to are skills you can pass on to others. You will be able to give specific examples of how these habits have helped you. You may think to yourself, "Why should I bother? It's up to other people to decide for themselves what they want to do in their lives." Well, how would you feel if the person you asked for help and support said, "No, I won't because there is nothing in it for me?"

Improving ourselves should be a lifelong pursuit, and one in which we can all help each other. At work, helping someone else might help you in the long run; perhaps you will need that person's assistance in doing a rush job. If others on your team have learned how to organize and plan their working life, they will be more willing and able to help out. As a manager or supervisor, you have a vested interest in helping your team members develop their skills because that helps the whole team to work more effectively.

Be generous!

For those of you who are parents, helping your children manage their time as youngsters will give them a headstart in life. It will enable them to achieve more and be successful, where other kids are left behind. It is a wonderful gift for any person you know, so be generous and give some of your precious time to help others make the most of their life. Time spent helping others to improve will have direct and indirect rewards for you as well.

Many organizations value people who take the time and have an interest in helping others. These often will be the ones picked for promotion or other interesting jobs, as they are seen as having a positive, "can-do" attitude and as people who take the initiative. Such people build good teams and to work with them to get jobs done on time and with a cheerful disposition.

Conclusion

This book on time management is like a journey. It has taken you through a number of different processes to help you manage your own time more effectively, thus releasing you from stress and overwork to enjoy a more balanced lifestyle. This will enable you to take part in many of the actions outside of work that are important to you, as well as helping you to be more in control of your job, rather than the other way round.

The processes you have encountered are self-assessment exercises meant to help you understand yourself better. Without that understanding, it is difficult to know where to begin. The reflection exercises were designed to help reinforce the learning about yourself, your work, and your life habits and to start you along the road to finding what else is important in your life. This understanding of what needs to change is followed by some principles to help you address areas in your life that you want to change. All of this is backed up by some practical examples, such as Action Plans and To-Do lists.

There will always be obstacles to what we want to achieve in our lives, because that is the way life is. However, further self-assessment in the form of understanding how you learn gives you more information about yourself that is both revealing and helpful. Such understanding adds another dimension about you, as a person, when viewed in the context of the rest of the learning from this book.

Finally, consider how you can help others in the pursuit of their life objectives and the part you can play as a coach who guides them through any improvements they would like to make. The encouragement you can give them, by recognizing their strengths and suggesting to them what they need to do to improve, will support them in their quest to improve other areas in their careers and life. They will always appreciate your contribution.

One final thought to use throughout your life: keep asking yourself, "What is really important?" Make it part of your daily routine. It will help you keep your priorities straight and remind you that you have a choice about what is the most important aspect of your life. By taking the time to check regularly with yourself about what is really important, you may find that some of the choices you have made are in conflict with your own stated goals. By asking yourself this question every day, you can ensure that both your actions and goals are in alignment, which will help you to make more conscious decisions.

Index

If you liked Time Management check out these career-building books from AMACOM.

Managing Multiple Bosses
How to Juggle Priorities, Personalities & Projects—and Make It Look Easy
Pat Nickerson

"Pat provides specific potential solutions to 'real world' problems…Once learned and practiced, these tools can provide the opportunity to evolve from feeling like a victim to being in control of your own destiny."
—*Dick Nettell, Senior Vice President, Procurement Services, Bank of America*

$15.95 ISBN: 0-8144-7025-4

Shortcuts for Smart Managers
Checklists, Worksheets, and Action Plans for Managers With No Time to Waste
Lisa Davis

Shortcuts for Smart Managers provides fast and easy access to the key principles of 30 essential management topics, from budgets and business ethics to the fine points of dealing with difficult people…from mastering the Internet to planning an event…from negotiating and selling to strategic planning…and more.

$24.95 ISBN: 0-8144-0432-4

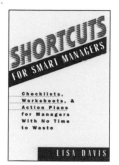

Get Organized!
Part of the Get-Ahead Toolkit Series
Bobbi Linkemer

Get Organized employs both a CD-ROM and a paperback book to show how to set goals, prioritize tasks, focus on results, create flexible to-do lists, manage time efficiently, arrange a workspace, organize electronic documents, deal with e-mail, and even clear off that desktop! It includes plenty of on-line worksheets.

$39.95 ISBN: 1-890003-01-8

The Time Trap
The Classic Book on Time Management
Alec Mackenzie

From the hands-down authority on time management techniques, here is a completely updated edition of the national bestseller. The Time Trap is filled with smart tactics, hard-hitting interviews, and handy time management tools to help you squeeze the optimal efficiency—and satisfaction—out of your workday.

$17.95 ISBN 0-8144-7926-X

Call 1-800-262-9699 or order in your local bookstore.